Your Guide Said What?
A Spirit Guide Q & A

Joan Hazel

Your Guide Said What?
A Spirit Guide Q & A

Myrddin Publishing

unique electronic & print books

unique electronic & print books

Copyright © 2015 by Joan Hazel

ISBN: 978-1-939296-94-8

Contents

Why I Wrote This Book

Your Guide Said What? is not a book designed to tell you how to contact your Spirit Guide. There happens to be many of those on the market and my guide thought doing another at this time was not the best use of his time.

What this book is designed to do is hopefully answer questions you may have about spirit guides, but were afraid to ask or didn't know who to ask.

Over the past 20 years I have grown more and more accustomed to working with my main guide, Marc. It is through working with him and my high council that I have come to appreciate my guides and their role in our lives. This is truly their book. I am merely the conduit for the information.

Acknowledgements

I would be remiss if I were to not give thanks to my dear friend Rebecca Robbearts for suggesting the topic of this book. I also want to give thanks to the Divine and my High Council for providing me with the information needed to complete this work.

Chapter 1

Spirit Guide Facts

What is a Spirit Guide?
A spirit guide is someone you made a contract with
when you were in pure energy form or spirit form
before you came to this plane of existence. They were
probably someone you knew in a past life or had a
strong connection with in the spirit realm.
It is the job of the spirit guide to help you in this
lifetime to steer through the obstacles and learn the
lessons that you have come here to learn.

I don't think I have a Guide.
Everyone has at least one spirit guide. It is
impossible to incarnate into this realm without one.
That would be the equivalent of an elementary
school sending a group of fourth graders on a field
trip without a chaperone.

Why can you hear them and I can't?
Everyone hears their guides although you may not
think of it as hearing. Their messages can come to us
in various ways. The difference is in the extent to

which we listen or pay attention. You might get a peculiar or gut feeling about something. Maybe you notice the same group of numbers or a word repeated over and over. In your mind this is a coincidence. (By the way, there is no such thing as a coincidence.) More times than not, this is your guide trying to get a message through to you.

On a side note: My husband swears he has no contact with his spirit guides. Yet he has evaded several life-threatening situations just by listening to his gut feeling. I truly believe this is how his spirit guide communicates with him.

How do they know what to help with?
When you first made the contract to come to this place, you, your main guide, and your higher council sat down and mapped out your life. Decisions were made as to the life lessons you were to learn, as well as, when and how certain people would come into your life. You may have even chosen specific obstacles as they would be part of the learning process for you.

So they will tell you what to do?
Not at all. It is not the place of guides to tell you what to do, nor are they allowed to do so. This is your life and you can make your own decisions.

Does everyone have the same number of guides?
Everyone does have at least one main guide or master guide. However, there is no set number of guides after that. Guides can come and go

throughout your life. They may stay for hours, days or years. Masters are guides that have ascended to a higher level or rank. A master guide may pop in and out, such as when you need comforting and support during a time of great sadness or severe illness.

What do you guides look like?
This is a simple question with a long answer, but I will try to shorten it. Think of all the different cultures and peoples that have existed over the millennia since time began and there you go. Since a guide is energy they can choose their appearance. This includes age, sex, hair color, eye color or any other characteristic you can think of.
Some guides will appear as they did in life, others will appear as they believe you would best accept them.

When Marc first appeared to me, I was a child. Because of my young age, Marc chose to shift his appearance into a little boy about my age. According to him, he did that so I wouldn't be scared. As I grew, he grew and aged in tune with me until I was an adult.

Now he chooses to appear to me as he looked when I knew him in a past life we shared. He has looked like this for more than 20 years, which is kind of irritating, since I continue to age and he remains in his early 30s.

What does your guide's voice sound like?
I can only think of a couple of times that I have physically heard my various guides' voices. In those times their voices were high-pitched and sometimes difficult to understand. Since guides vibrate on a much higher frequency their voice can almost sound like a chirp or Mickey Mouse.

That is why I prefer telepathy. Telepathy is easier on the guide because they do not have to slow down their vibration. The words sound in my mind as thoughts or sometimes images. If I do receive a full sentence (which is rare) the vocal timbre is closer to normal. As you learn to work with your guides you will discover the best form of communication to use.

Do all guides have the same personality?
Do all people on the planet Earth have the same personality? Just as you can have five different personalities within a family the same can be said for your guides.
I have three guides that spend most of their time with me. All three have different personalities. Marc has a very dry sense of humor. Constantine is incredibly stoic and never smiles. Christoph, on the other hand, is always smiling and often cracks jokes, but no matter their personality, guides always have your best interest at heart and will never say or do anything that would harm you.

Can your guides be a deceased family member or friend?
As much as this answer is going to hurt some people the answer is no. Since spirit guides, especially the main guide, are with you from birth they can not be someone you have known in this lifetime.
That is not to say passed loved ones cannot help you in this life. They can, but they will not be your main guide.

What if my guide tells me something negative?
Your main guide has been with you since birth and will be with you until your passing. They will never do anything to hurt you or put you in harms way, nor will they ask you to do anything that would ever hurt others. Even the guides that come and go throughout your life will never speak negatively to you.
Hear me well when I say this. If your guide says anything to you that is harmful, detrimental, or disrespectful in anyway, then that **is not** your guide.

How do you know your guide's name?
The best way to know your guide's name is to ask. The first name that comes to mind, no matter how strange it sounds, is probably it. I shortened Marc's name because when he first began working with me I had a hard time understanding Greek and at the time, it was difficult for me to pronounce.
I will tell you though it really doesn't matter what you call them. According to Marc I could've just as easily called him Bubba and he still would've

answered. Our guides are not overly concerned with what you call them, they are just happy you have taken the opportunity to acknowledge them. Personally, I do believe it best if you keep the male names with male guides and female names with female guides.

How do you know whether your guide is male or female?

Once again, all you have to do is ask. Your first answer is right. Try not to second guess these things. As a general rule you will have the same sexed guide as what you are. However, that is not 100% accurate. For instance most all of my guides are male energies. I have been told this is not the norm. Occasionally, I will have a female guide pop in for a week or two then pop out again.

Can you have a guide that is homosexual?

Not really, but let me explain. Guides are made of pure energy meaning they do not have a physical form. Therefore do not have the same physical desires or needs that those of us in the corporeal realm have. Because of this they do not consider themselves either heterosexual or homosexual. However, they will always come to you with the personality and characteristics that best work with you. So if for some reason you are more comfortable with someone whose mannerisms and personality align with someone who is homosexual, then your guide will do so.

Can you change your main guide?

Short answer — yes. However, this is not commonplace, but I have known of this happening in a few cases. I have actually had one of my higher council members removed. To do so actually takes a lot of discussion and mediation between your higher self, your guides, and the higher council. In my case, I actually had someone who was able to intercede on my behalf.

Do guides watch you all the time?

This seems to be a huge concern for some people. Your guides could watch you all the time, but they don't. According to Marc you can rest assured our guides don't stand around like a bunch of voyeurs taking notes and chatting about us around the water cooler. Besides they actually see more of an energy field than the 3-D imaging we see.

What about when you are in the bathroom?

As I stated above, yes they could see you if they chose to do so, but I cannot remind you enough that your guides have been here since the day you came into this world. They have seen you at your best and at your worst, so take this information and make your own decision.

If the thought of them seeing you naked is something you are worried about then set this as a boundary. Ask them to stay away when you need the privacy, and they will respect your wishes. Many of us work through telepathy so having a guide in the room with you is not always necessary.

Can they see you having sex?
This is a big ole no. As Marc said, "Why would we want to?"
He also tells me that during those intimate times a type of energetic force field or shield actually comes up around you and your partner so even if they wanted to they would be unable to do so.

Do your guides talk to each other?
Yes, guides do speak with each other. They will have conversations about how best to serve and help you. Think of it like this. Your higher council works a lot like a board of directors. You are their client and the various other guides in your spiritual life work underneath them with your main guide working as upper management. The other guides assist with him or her to insure that you, their client, receive all the benefits the board has to offer by giving status updates, strategic planning, etc.
In the same way a board of directors wants only the best for their company or industry, your board of directors wants only the best for you.

Do my guides talk to other people's guides?
I have often accused my guides of hanging out with the guides of my friends swapping war stories. The council assures me this is not the case, but that the guides of people who are friends, partners, and coworkers do speak with each other, especially if you are working toward a single cause or goal.
I know that I have physically heard mine and my husband's guide speaking with each other. I was

almost asleep at the time and their mumbling woke me. Unfortunately, when they realized I was eavesdropping they went into super-ninja stealth mode. I guess whatever they were discussing was not for me to know.

Message from Marc

The beauty of being human is that humans have free will. The beauty of the symbiotic relationship with your guide is that they are there to guide and support you. They cannot tell you what to do such as which job to take. In the end, you will do whatever you want.

It matters not the number of warning bells and whistles we send your way, you can be quite stubborn creatures.

A guide can make you feel ill when a decision is not in your best interest. They can also distract you enough you may forget to make a turn while driving or have you stop because you "just need to get a cup of coffee". Then, when you get back on the road, you pass a wreck, and realize if you hadn't stopped for those 10 minutes, you could of been part of that pile up. Ever said to yourself: I should've listened to my gut on that one or I knew it, I just didn't listen? More than likely that gut intuition was your guide giving you instructions. We will give you the information; it is up to you to listen.

Chapter 2

Guide Types

Just as there are different jobs within any company structure, our guides have different occupations where we are concerned. I will briefly describe a few here. This is by no means a complete list, but it will give you an idea of the variations.

What is the Master or High Council?
This is a group guides who are on a higher evolutionary or ascended plane. Usually your master/high council is made up of two to three council members. This is not to be confused with the guides that come and go throughout your life. You can also have a main guide that is not a member of the Master Council.

I will tell you that having more than two or three high council members is not one of those times you can consider "the more the merrier". I actually had a four member council and it was extremely noisy and often confusing.

Main or Master Guide

A main guide is the guide or possibly guides, in some instances, which work with you consistently. They have been with you since the beginning and will be with you until the end. Rarely do they leave your side and you can call upon them at any time. I read somewhere that different people can share a main guide. According to my council, that is not quite accurate.

A guide may momentarily step in to help another soul, but he will not take on another as his main charge. This is possible because as pure energy, a guide can be in multiple places.

There is a **Guide of Protection** who basically works as your spiritual gatekeeper and body guard. This guide will help to psychically shield you and protect you when needed. My spiritual bodyguard just popped in one day. He was a Templar Knight and is quick to pull his sword when I need extra protection.

However, I have learned that there are times that I need more protection than he can give and that is when I call upon the angels for more shielding.

There is a group of guides that I call the **Technical Consultants.** These guides are unique to you and will match the life purpose you have here in this realm. If you are creative, then there may be a guide that helps with that artistic or musical part of you. If you work more in the technical arena, then it is highly possible your guide will also be technically minded.

The last of the groups I will mention are what I term the **Revolving Guides**. These guides will come to you for a specific reason and once that lesson is learned or situation is resolved they move on to help others. Examples of a revolving guide would be a muse type guide that aids in the creation of music, art or literature.

Chapter 3

Angels As Guides

Although the main purpose of this book is to cover the realm of spirit guides, I would be remiss if I did not at least touch on the subject of angels as guides.

Do you consider angels to be spirit guides?
No, guardian angels and spirit guides are not the same although their jobs are similar.

The differences are:

1. Angels have never incarnated and lived as human, where as spirit guides have so angels cannot be considered spirit guides. Yet they are guides within their own right.

2. Since angels have not lived as human, they have a higher vibrational frequency than do spirit guides. This gives angels a white glow or aura, where as some may see guides as a bluish white.

However, I will add that there have been humans who have ascended to Archangel status. They are: Archangel Metatron who is referred to in the

Christian Bible as Enoch and Archangel Sandalphon who was once Elijah.

What is a Guardian Angel?
A guardian angel is the angel assigned to you from the time of your birth until the time of your death. It is the job of your guardian angel to make certain that you are safe.

How do you know if you've met one?
Guardian angels can temporarily appear to us in human form in times of great stress or when protection is needed. However you may never know you encountered one. You may only sense that there was something not quite human about them.

I have been told that one characteristic of angels is that they do not communicate audibly. Instead they will give you a sense or feeling through telepathy. For example, you would not hear the words "everything will be all right", you would simply feel the sense of relief and the words may appear as a thought inside your head.

Can a deceased loved one be your Guardian Angel?
No. As much as we would love to believe it possible, humans do not ascend to become an angel. A deceased loved one can be a lower level guide of sorts.

Do Guardian Angels protect you?
Most definitely yes. That is one of their main jobs! Think of all the stories you have heard about being involved in horrible accidents where they should

have died. Instead they were rescued by a stranger who disappeared as soon as the person was safe.

Growing up in Tennessee, thunderstorms and tornados were the norm. It was during one of these particularly nasty storms that the screen and glass door on the front of our house blew open. I rushed to grab the door to pull it back into place.

Before I was able to reach the door, the wind blew the door shut shattering the door and sending chards of glass flying around me. I can remember freezing in place, unable to speak or move until the whole thing was over. I should have been cut to ribbons. Instead, I was without a scratch. To this day I am convinced my guardian angel surrounded me in that moment, keeping me from harm.

Guardian angels are our protectors, helpers, and guides. However, humans have free will. Both guardian angels and spirit guides are trained to respect that. Our guardian angels and helper angels will never tell us what to do or make our decisions for us. They also will not interfere unless we ask for their intercession except in the case of a life or death situation.

Chapter 4

Other Entities As Guides

Can animals be guides instead of people?
Animals can and are great helper guides. They can come to you in dreams or visions when you meditate. You may also notice that a particular animal or insect appears frequently around you. When this happens ask yourself what is this animal trying to tell me? What characteristics of this creature may I need to incorporate into my life at this time?

One other thing about animal guides. Most all of us have an animal we are drawn to or have an affinity for. I consider this to be your main animal guide or totem, and it is the qualities of that animal that you will be more in line with.

Just as human guides will come and go throughout your life so it will be with animal guides. There are many books written on the magic and use of animal spirits plus you can normally or readily find that information on the Internet.

What about aliens?
Both this question and its answer surprised me, but according to my guide an alien can be a spirit guide.

Marc's explanation is as follows: At our core we are all sentient or responsive energy before we were incarnated into this life, and it is to that energy we shall return in its pure form once we have left this plane of existence. With this is mind it should stand to reason that aliens are also made of energy and can be a guide. In fact there are beings from other solar systems and realms that have decided to incarnate on this plane as a human. So yes, you can have a guide that can be considered an alien.

What about fairies and elementals?
Although it is possible to see and even communicate with fairies and elementals, they are at their essence close to the earthy realm, placing their vibration too low which is why they cannot be considered part of the spiritual realm. Also, and I will have to ask forgiveness for this comment, but the Fey are too mischievous and often too self-serving to ever be a guide.

What about other mythical creatures such as unicorns or dragons?
I know this may seem strange, but dragons, unicorns and even griffins can be guides. Much like the answer to the alien question I was shocked at this. In fact, I asked my guide and the high council about this multiple times just so I could be positive I received the correct information.

Marc reminded me of the client I had with a revolving guide that at the time was a beautiful, baby dragon. The dragon was no more than 10 to 12 inches long, with iridescent purple, blue and turquoise scales. The dragon spent most the reading flying behind the client's head doing loops and back flips. At first I was confused since I had never seen anything like that before.

Despite my apprehension, I asked my client if this made sense to her, she told me she understood perfectly what I was talking about. She just wasn't sure why she should have a baby dragon as a guide. The message I received was that the dragon was there to show her not to take life so seriously and to have more fun. What a great lesson and what an even greater guide to show her.

Can your guides shift their form?
Yes. As stated before your guides are made up of pure energy and can therefore change their shape taking on a form that you will be comfortable interacting with.

Closing Thoughts
As I finished this chapter, my high council was adamant I add this warning:

There are many people who are drawn to what are often considered dark images such as vampires. My guides want me to let you know it would be in your best interest to be leery if a guide showed themselves or allowed their energy to morph into any creature whose core being is one of darkness. Vampires are best known for stealing a person's life-force. It doesn't matter how much of a romantic, leading man or woman spin Hollywood puts on their story.

Remember that your guides and angels are pure, unconditional love. They come from a source of light so to appear in any other way would be impossible.

Chapter 5

Ghosts Verses Spirits

Is there a difference between a Ghost and a Spirit? If so, what is that difference?
For many people the terms ghost and spirit are used interchangeably. For them they are one and the same, but my understanding is that a ghost is a spirit, but a spirit is not necessarily a ghost. Let me explain.

Spirit means one's spiritual body as opposed to the physical 3-D body that we live in. While we are incarnated upon this plane of existence we are all made up of the spirit essence and the physical.

A spirit or spirit form in the instance of ghost hunting or working in the world of mediumship is the spirit essence of someone who has passed on from this world. My understanding is when one is a spirit it can come and go of its own free will and is not bound to this world.

A ghost, on the other hand, is a spirit who is earthbound. They are the ones responsible for hauntings. Some do not comprehend or accept the fact they are dead and should move on. Some do understand and yet, for whatever reason, refuse to move on.

Can a ghost hurt you?

I have always been told that a ghost cannot hurt the living since the living has dominion in the physical realm. However, they can cause you to hurt yourself out of fear. The ones that seem to get a great deal of publicity on the ghost hunting television shows or that are written about that scratch or inflict pain on the living are not ghosts. These entities are something entirely different. In some religions they are referred to as demons.

Do demons exist? Can they cause you harm?

Short answer—yes, demons do exist, but I need to make a clarification here. To the best of my knowledge, demons are not the minions of Satan or the Devil. Instead they are malevolent, sentient, non-corporeal beings. They can attach themselves to humans wreaking all levels of chaos, and can cause both physical and mental harm.

Chapter 6

Forms of
Psychic Communication

Although this book is not about being psychic for clarification I will touch on the different types of psychic abilities that can be used when speaking with your guides. As stated earlier, this book is not a "how to" on contacting your guides. There are many of those available.

Clairaudience
Clairaudience is defined as clear hearing. This can be done in two ways.

1. Subjective Clairaudience is when you hear a voice or sounds internally. These often sound like they could be your own thoughts, and sometimes it is hard to distinguish which is you and which is them. The best way is by pronoun use. When saying: I need to go to the market — that is your consciousness. If you hear the words: You need to go to the market, more than likely that is a guide.

Once when I was working with my guide, I asked him how I was to know it was my thoughts or ones coming from him. In the most matter-of-fact voice I heard, "When you think wow that guy is hot, I promise that is not me."

2. Objective Clairaudience is the ability to physically hear sounds, and more than one person can hear those sounds.

After a shopping trip, my husband and I were bringing in the groceries. My husband quickly walked through the den and the kitchen, not stopping until he reached my office. When I asked him what was wrong, he said he heard two men talking in the house and was afraid someone had broken into our home. I too had heard the voices, but it was common for me to do so and it shocked me that he had since he had never expressed having experienced anything like that before.

There are many biblical and historical figures reported to have clairaudience. A few who come to come to mind are Joan of Arc, Hidegard von Bingen, and Moses. As I have discussed earlier my guides and I have developed a subjective clairaudience. Rarely do they use conjunctions, articles, or complete sentences. For example: I will receive the words "red ball" as opposed to "the ball is red".

Clairsentience
Clairsentience is the ability of clear sensing or clear knowing. Many people call this using their intuition. It is being able to sense things that are unseen. It is having a gut feeling about a situation or hunch. For Peter Parker, his spidey senses tingled. For you it

may be the experience of goose flesh or an
unexplainable inner knowing.

Clairvoyance
Clairvoyance or clear seeing is being able to see
things with your third eye, not your physical eyes.
You can see symbols, auras, items or past or present
events. When doing readings from others I have seen
all types of symbols and even scenes from movies.

Telepathy
Telepathy is a form of communication that takes
place between separate minds. This communication
can be in the form of words, images or feelings.

Psychometry
Psychometry is the ability for a person to sense or
read the history of an object by touching or holding
the object. This is due to the vibrational energy that
has been embedded in the object. I have never
personally experienced psychometry to the extent of
seeing or sensing the history of an object. I have felt
vibrations in an object when perusing an antique
store or flea market.

Scrying
Scrying is the practice of using a reflective,
translucent or luminescent object, in the hopes of
seeing or peeking into the spiritual world. Think of
every picture you have seen of a fortune teller with a
crystal ball. They are using scrying to receive their

information. However there are many other tools one can use such as crystals, stones, glass, mirrors, water, fire, or smoke.

Dowsing

Dowsing is using a tool or instrument other than a part of your body to receive answers. One of the most common tools used for this would be a pendulum. When you first begin using your pendulum you will want to program it, by asking your guides to show you yes, no, maybe, etc.
Side note: When using any form of communication with the spirit world, always protect/shield yourself and ask that your answers come solely from the divine, your high council, or higher self.
Once again, there are multiple books and websites where you can find more information about the use of pendulums.

Dreams

Dreams are frequently used by guides to give you messages and are a great place to see your guides. In fact, I have only quasi-seen what my guide looks like in dreams. I hope that one day he will appear to me when I am awake. Guides, much like angels exist in a higher vibrational plane than we do so for us to see them they must slow their vibrational frequency enough to actually manifest. We also have to raise our vibrational frequency so the variation in speed is not that different.

Ouija Boards/Spirit Board

Ouija boards are flat boards with letters, numbers and a few words written on it. A planchette or heart shaped piece of wood or plastic is placed in the center of the board. The participants place the tips of their fingers on the planchette and ask their questions. The planchette will move around the board pointing to the letters, numbers, or words to spell out messages.

I add this form of communication only because I know mediums and spiritualists who will use a spirit board to communicate with their guides. Personally I am against a novice using this form of communication.

Most users of Ouija boards will pick up one thinking it is a game, after all it is sold as one, but I assure you a spirit board is not a toy and should not be used as one.

If you choose to use a spirit board, and I cannot stress this enough, please be sure to ground yourself and set a sacred space of protection around you and any others that will be participating with you. Again be sure to ask that your answers come solely from the divine, the highest source of love and light.

My guides were resolute in my telling you that if you do not protect yourself when dealing with a spirit board, the possibility exists to contact the good, the bad, and anything in between.

Channeling

Channeling is when a person serves as the conduit of spirit communication by allowing the spirit to take over and control the physical body. Some call it possession and technically it is since the spirit possesses the body.

This isn't exactly once of my favorite things to do since I do not like having no control of my surroundings. The only form of channeling I have participated in is automatic writing. Although there is an argument to be made that anytime messages from the spirit world are received we are channeling. I would have to disagree since in other forms of communication you still have control of your faculties.

Automatic Writing

Automatic writing is when a spirit guide is allowed to use your body to write their messages to you. Some might even consider this a form of channeling since the guide is using you.

I have used automatic writing once or twice. The only word of wisdom I can give you here is be prepared to write quickly, forget everything you know about spelling and grammar, and expect to decipher some horrible penmanship. It is not you doing the writing. You are merely the instrument so do not filter your thoughts or contemplate what you think your handwriting should look like. If you do, both you and your guide will become frustrated.

Chapter 7

Miscellaneous Q & A

How do you know when your guides are near or communicating with you?
This question has many answers. For me, I get a tingling sensation on the top of my head like little sparks of electricity running across the crown of my head or sometimes there is a pressure in the center of my forehead where my third eye is located, although this has been happening less and less.

Often there is loud ringing in my ear. When that happens I call it a download. A download is when your guides or angels are giving you messages that come so quickly and with such intensity that they go directly into your subconscious to be accessed at a later date.

When you begin to work with your guides you may also notice a feeling of someone touching your cheek. Some even liken it to having a spider web across their face.

What do I do with the information I receive if it does not pertain to me?

Once you become comfortable in communicating with your guides, you may get a message that is intended for someone else. If this does happen it is up to you whether or not to share the information.

What do I do if I get messages that make no sense?

There is a lot of information floating in the ethos, and once you get attuned to hearing those messages, you might accidentally tap into something that has no benefit for you. If this happens, then I suggest you ask your guides to not give you information unless it is something you are able to understand and use.

What if my child talks to imaginary friends? Are they talking to their guides?

If your child happens to be gifted with any form of psychic ability, they could be picking up on their guides or any other spirit form that maybe in your home or simply visiting. To find out which it is, you may want to seek the help of a reputable or trusted psychic/medium.

What if I know it is my child's guide, but their presence scares my child?

In the case where your child may be frightened of their guide or a visiting spirit, kindly ask the guide not to show themselves or speak to your child until such time as the child is old enough to handle the interaction.

Please note that the guide has not left or abandoned your child. They are simply working in the background.

Arguing With Your Guides
I wish I could say this doesn't happen, but it does. I have argued with them and will probably do so again. However, I have had disagreements with them since the beginning. Mostly this has happened when I get a message that needs to be delivered to someone else. Sometimes I have balked at giving the message arguing that the unknowing recipient may not want to be disturbed. Eventually though I will give in and do as the guides request.

In those times that I haven't listened, things turn out not so great. Of course, this is when I get a snarky comment such as "how did that work out for you?" or I feel him roll his eyes at me.

I have become frustrated to the point I must ask him to walk away and let me think. Once I cool off, I apologize and things go back to the way they were. I have been told that arguing or disagreeing with your guides is a no-no by other spiritualist and healers. But to me, if your guides are your friends, then you can treat them as such.

The DiNozzo Affect

Those of you who watch NCIS will understand what I am talking about. For those that don't, I apologize.

Sometimes we humans don't want to listen to our guides. We will beg them for answers or help with a situation. Unless it is something you are not supposed to know, they will always answer you. The problem is we don't always like the answer we're getting (remember freewill?) .So we ignore all the gentle signs and symbols that our guides send us. Still we keep asking. Still we keep getting the same answer.

Please understand that our guides are tenacious and tolerant of our constant asking, up to a point. This is when they will give you a psychic slap in the back of the head. By that I mean you will have something huge happen that pushes you in the right direction.

The best example I can give you of this is when I quit my job. For months I had been asking for a sign as to whether I should stay in a job where the money was okay, but I wasn't happy. Everyday I asked for signs and every few days something would happen to point me in the right direction. Out of fear, I would tell myself I misunderstood, or that I really didn't see what I think I saw.

The day came when they realized I was not going to listen, and they had to take drastic measures. That was the day I quit my job. As I often say, I was pushed off the imaginary cliff without the aid of an imaginary parachute.

I heard the words "I quit" as they flowed from my lips. I felt the physical vibrations of my voice as I said them. The thing was, I didn't say them, and it wasn't until I was sitting in the car, my belongings in hand, that I wondered what had happened.

This reminds me of the adage: be careful what you ask for because you just might get it. And let me add that sometimes the process can be a painful one.

Show your Guide Love
Your guides, like you, need to feel love and appreciation. To show this you can do something as simple as saying thank you, include them in your prayers or if you perform any type of energy work such as Reiki, send that to them also.

Message From Marc

Please remember we are called spirit guides, not spirit controllers or spirit bosses. It is our job to guide and support, not tell you what to do. As I often remind my charge, humans have free will which means they have their opinions and will make their own decisions.

We are also the best friends you can and will ever have. We know everything there is to know about you. When you are happy, we are happy for you. When you are sad, we are sad for you. We will even allow you to disagree and argue with us, and the best part, we do not take your anger personally and will not leave you because of it.

About The Author

Joan Hazel is a Reiki Master, Certified Toe Reader and Soul Coach. In addition she is a best-selling author of paranormal fantasy: The Last Guardian, Book One of the Guardian Series and Burdens of a Saint, Book Two of the Guardian Series.

Hazel is a native of Corinth, Mississippi and currently resides in Deland, Florida with her husband and their two dogs, Izzy and Ellie.
Learn more about Joan at www.joanhazel.com

Other Books By Joan Hazel

The Last Guardian

Burdens of a Saint

What the Heart Sees

One Last Thing...

If you enjoyed this book or have questions, I'd love to hear from you. I would also be grateful if you'd post a short review on Amazon. Your support really does make a difference and I read all the reviews personally so I can get your feedback and make this book even better.

Thanks again for your support!